refresh

A **Not-So-New** Guide to Being Church and Doing Life

Michael Moynagh & Rob Peabody

MONARCH
BOOKS

Oxford UK, and Grand Rapids, USA

Text copyright © 2016 Michael Moynagh and Rob Peabody
Design and illustrations © 2016 David Uribe
This edition copyright © 2016 Lion Hudson

The right of Michael Moynagh and Rob Peabody to be
identified as the authors of this work has been asserted by
them in accordance with the Copyright, Designs and Patents
Act 1988.

Published by Monarch Books
an imprint of
Lion Hudson plc
Wilkinson House, Jordan Hill Road,
Oxford OX2 8DR, England
Email: monarch@lionhudson.com
www.lionhudson.com/monarch

ISBN 978 0 85721 765 3

First edition 2016

Book cover and illustrations by David Uribe – daviduribe.com

A catalogue record for this book is available from the British
Library

Printed and bound in Slovenia, March 2016, LH48

Contents

Jesus died so that you may be forgiven and inherit eternal life.
Jesus died to set you free.
Jesus died so that you may experience abundant life.
Jesus died to give you peace, rest, fulfilment... everything you were originally created to experience.
Jesus died so that you don't have to.
Jesus died to bring you home.
Jesus died for **you**.

//

For many of us this is where the story stops. This is our practical, lived-out theology.
The Gospel ends and starts with **you**.

//

What if we have it mixed up? What if we lost what it is all about somewhere along the way?
What if **you** got in the way?

//

What if God and His story didn't begin and end with you?
What if God was up to something even bigger?

//

And what if God was inviting **you** into it?

1

1

Why this matters

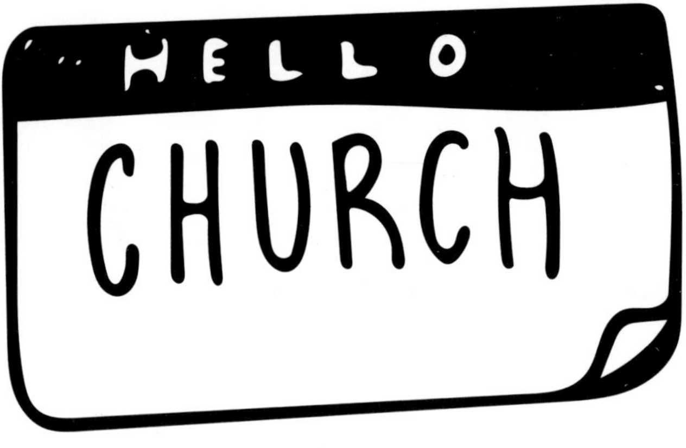
HELLO
CHURCH

This book is about not simply going to church, but being the church.

It's about doing life in a way that takes full advantage of the invitation Jesus gave to you in His resurrection.

What a topic, right?

I know it sounds complex and daunting, but give us the next 29 minutes of your time and we promise to get you pointed in the right direction.

What Jesus wants for you and your Christian life is not complicated. It is not top-shelf academic theory with confusing language. It's actually really simple – a gift anyone can receive.

So grab a drink, find a quiet place, and forego one television show. Invest 29 minutes with Jesus to unwrap what could change your priorities forever.

What did Jesus intend when he came to earth?

Let's start at the beginning

As you read the Gospel accounts of His life, time and again you see Jesus showing, explaining, and telling what it looks like to be part of the Kingdom of God. His life models it, His words describe it, and His actions exemplify what it means to live for God's Kingdom. Then, through His death and resurrection, He provides a way for all people throughout all time to join Him in this Kingdom way of life.

And to bring it to others.

That's one of the most interesting parts of the story. When Jesus returns to heaven, He leaves an unusual goodbye. He tells His followers that once He's gone, His Spirit will come to the community that has gathered around Him and fill it with power to witness to the entire world.

This makes the picture of what Jesus has been up to a bit clearer… God has sent Jesus on a mission to the earth, now Jesus is sending His people to do the same.

Jesus' short life leaves in its wake not a new book, not a building, not a religious system, but a community with Jesus inside it – a community that will introduce Jesus and His Kingdom to the world.

Jesus is not inviting you to be an onlooker, a casual Christian. He wants you to be immersed in His community – for a purpose, which is to help share the Kingdom with others. Through you, He wants others to see that the Kingdom is brimming with kindness, animated by justice, passionate about the environment, and flooded with the presence of Jesus.

The Father has made you unique and gifted you supernaturally to play a distinct role in bringing this Kingdom of love to other people's doorsteps.

Here's what you need to know

Something remarkable is happening today. A new movement is quickly gaining traction and influence across the West and is spreading to the global South. It is called "fresh expressions of church".

The funny thing about the name is that in one sense the movement is completely fresh, but in another it is actually not fresh at all.

Let us explain.

You may have heard of missional communities, church plants, organic church, pub church, or new monastic communities, all of which are names to describe a "non-traditional" church.

You know traditional churches – the ones with a building, a steeple, and a door for all the people (who, by the way, in most western contexts, aren't attending in huge numbers). Well, these fresh expressions are very different. They emerge among homeless people, the residents of an apartment block, users of a laundromat, people learning English, people on the beach (there are over 300 surfing churches in Brazil!), and in the workplace – wherever people hang out and do life.

These small groups of Christians are igniting explosions of love all over the world.

They prayerfully find ways to serve the people around them, they build community with those involved, they share Jesus with anyone who is interested, and they encourage church to take shape around individuals coming to faith.

These new Christian communities are not stepping-stones to an existing church. Because fewer and fewer people are seeking out the traditional churches, they are church for people right where they are – in the middle of everyday life.

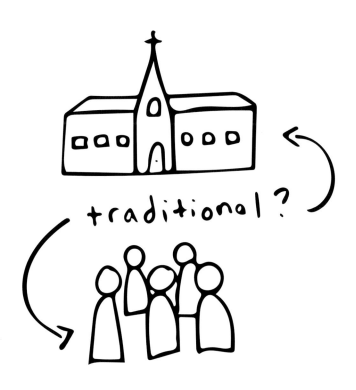

traditional ?

They are called "fresh expressions of church" – a term covering any form of non-traditional church that is working outside of traditional church buildings and services to focus on reaching and serving a lost world.

So, in one sense, they are absolutely fresh because they are popping up in different types of ways and in all sorts of new places. More on this in the following chapters…

But in another sense, these "new" types of churches are not fresh at all! They are throwbacks to the first century and to the earliest churches on record. These first churches actually met in people's homes.

Now homes were the epicentre of everyday life – of family life, of networks, and often of work. Half the homes excavated at ancient Pompeii have workshops, horticultural plots, or some other form of work attached to them. So these churches were right at the heart of ordinary life.

The first Christians lived in close proximity to one another, shared what they had, knew and allowed themselves to be known by one another, prayed and celebrated together, studied God's teachings together, served the people around them, and were open to **anyone** joining in with them.[1] This is what they called church.

It was so different and inviting, and people on the outside so loved what they saw, that ***every day*** the number in the Christian community grew as God added those who were being saved.[2]

The church was truly transformational, not only for the people involved, but for their friends and neighbours. Indeed, entire cities were disrupted because of how the people of "The Way" lived.[3] These Christians impacted and disrupted for God the commerce, religion, lifestyle, arts, and social structures of the day by acting out Jesus in their day-to-day lives.

The church that we read about in the book of Acts was a fresh expression. In fact, it was the freshest expression the world had ever seen. Through Jesus, God was doing something entirely new.

The church was not like the synagogue; it was not like the temple that people simply went to week in and week out. It was completely new because it brought to the world for the first time communal life with Jesus – a community absolutely committed to serving people on the outside. The church was a gift, not to Christians but to the world.

So when we refer to "fresh expressions of church", we are speaking of something that is ancient, yet immediately significant now.

They are relevant to you

The ideas behind fresh expressions have the power to re-calibrate your experience of church. They will open up radically different ways for you to meet Jesus.

Might it be that you and the believers you know need a bit of shaking up?

Has church-as-usual become stagnant, lifeless, or uneventful as you clock in and out week after week?

Is your Christian life drudging along, a slave to the status quo? Do you ever find yourself asking, "There's got to be more, right?"

If any of this sounds remotely familiar…

Then it might be time to get back to what Jesus started, time to re-imagine your role in the great story of God and His Kingdom, time to discover with fresh eyes what the Spirit may be calling you into, time to journey into the Father's intentions – for you.

How would you describe your current church or Christian community?

In what ways do you think the early church differed from today's traditional church?

Do you feel like your life with Jesus needs a bit of shaking up? If so, what are your biggest hindrances to living the abundant Kingdom life Jesus speaks of?

What do you think is the difference between going to church and being the church?

2

Five things you need to know

Here are five things that you must know if you are to be church as you do life:

#1. God is missional and wants us prayerfully to join him

This is one of the big themes of Scripture. God's mission – his salvation plan – is to bring creation to perfection (see Genesis 12:3; John 3:17; Revelation 21: 1–4).

Mission has always been vital to God… from the very beginning. The Father did not just wake up one day and say on a whim, "You know, mission might be a cool thing to do." There's no way He would do that, because God's character is the same yesterday, today, and forever (Hebrews 13:8). In fact, there is no before and after when it comes to God. So logically, there cannot be a time when God was not missional and then a time when He is.

Mission, therefore, is not a second step for God. It's the first one.

It's who He is.

So, logically, it cannot be a second step for Christians, who are imitators of God. Mission must be a priority, not an afterthought. Fresh expressions of church are a significant approach to mission.

#2. God wants mission to be done by communities in life

We are not meant to do mission alone, but together – like the Father, Son, and Holy Spirit. Jesus, for example, was constantly in touch with His Father (John 8:28) and was led by the Spirit (Luke 4:1). They do it together… in community.

Jesus also did mission in community with His disciples – in the middle of everyday life. When He taught His disciples how to do mission, He sent them in pairs – in community – to the villages and towns, to ordinary places where ordinary life was taking place (Luke 9:1ff; 10:1ff).

The first churches were in people's homes, which were the epicentre of family, society, and often work. These communities were witnesses to the Jesus way of life in their day-to-day. Fresh expressions of church follow this example. They are communities for mission in the everyday.

These communities on mission for God proclaim to the rest of the world the time when Jesus will ultimately fill "all things" – in all compartments and sectors of life (Ephesians 1:23). One day, He will be in every part of existence.

LegacyXS at a skateboard park is one example of how fresh expressions point to this future and make Christ's body, the church, visible in every segment of society.[4]

#3. Fresh expressions offer the gift of being community with Jesus

The best gifts are those that suit the recipient – it's good to know what they like and appreciate. Would a bottle of wine be much of a gift if the recipient were teetotal? It's exactly the same with this gift.

Offering community appropriately to a friend could mean inviting them to an existing church. But there is no one size fits all community for people, for some, they will need something different.

Imagine that a church meets in a time and place that are hard to reach, and in a style that is inaccessible. The church won't be a gift if it can't be reached. In these cases, the gift of the church will take the form of a new community with Jesus – a new expression of church that's available to them in their circumstances. The church must adapt to be a relevant gift for those to whom Jesus offers it.

Saturday Gathering, for instance, offers Christian community to clients of a food bank who find existing congregations practically or culturally inaccessible.[5]

Fresh expressions beautifully echo Holy Communion: a piece of the church is broken off to become a new community, which is shared with others.

#4. Fresh Expressions are a rounded form of mission

They hold together the Great Commandment (to love others) and the Great Commission (to make disciples). Jesus combined the two and so did the early church, which cared for the poor alongside sharing the gospel. It was a naturally supernatural combination.

Fresh expressions unite both today. Many start with loving service – from providing a place to chat, to passing on skills, to working with homeless people.

Community is formed with those being served; individuals are introduced to Jesus if they are so inclined, and something with the shape and character of church begins to emerge.

The aim is to see individuals – and their neighbourhoods and networks – transformed by the Spirit.

#5. Fresh expressions work — numerically!

Over 3,500 have been started in the UK across the denominations. Research suggests that in 2014 they existed in 13.5 per cent of Church of England parishes.

And here's the best part: their leaders reported that three quarters of people attending came from outside the church.[6] Most of those attending are entering the Kingdom community for the first time.

All in all, fresh expressions are helping to grow the Kingdom by strengthening the church's mission.

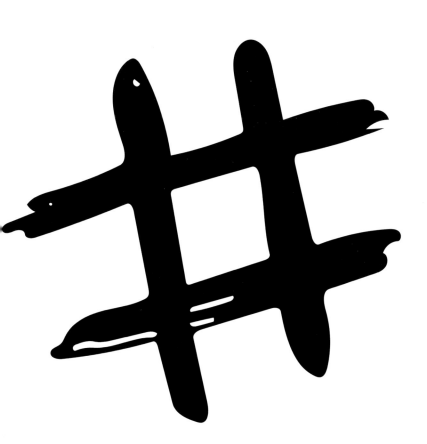

25

Have you ever thought about church being a gift to people? Think about your friends for a moment. What would be the most relevant gift the church could give to them?

Why do so many people think mission is optional?

Do you have any friends that you do mission with? List their names here.

What is your next step as a community in doing mission together?

3

What are fresh expressions of church?

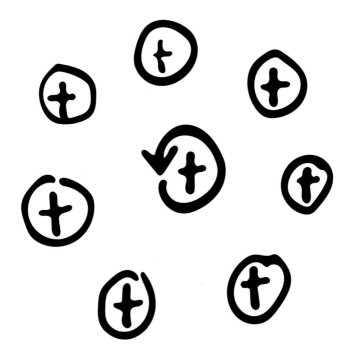

Fresh expressions are catching on across all streams of the church in the Western world. So much so, that in the UK's largest denomination, the Church of England, one in eight local churches have started such an initiative.[7]

But what exactly are they?

At their core, fresh expressions of church have a few essentials. They are missional, contextual, formational and ecclesial.

In other words, they:

- Care for and serve people *outside the church*.
- *Adapt to the context*. They listen to the people they serve and enter their worlds.
- *Form disciples*. They journey with people to people to discover and become more like Jesus.
- *Express church* where life happens. They are not bridges to an existing church, but a form of church for others in the midst of their lives.

Here's an example…

Three Christian women in a small town loved cooking. They invited teenagers over to their homes to learn how to cook — and then eat what they'd made. As they ate together, they informally talked about their lives, and, when it seemed natural, the women shared what their Christian faith meant to them.

These meals always started with a prayer. The teenagers were invited to add what they were thankful for and the requests they might have. The girls would write their prayers on a piece of paper, drop them into a cooking bowl, and then pass the bowl around drawing out a prayer to read.

Increasingly, the teenagers chatted about and explored Christianity, and eventually "Cook @ Chapel", a new Christian community, was born.

Similar groups are now forming elsewhere.[8]

Fresh expressions have many names. You may hear them called missional communities, organic church, church plants, café church, new monastic communities, alternative congregations, gatherings, discipleship groups – almost anything! They come in many diverse shapes and sizes, but always reflect their context. They are completely relevant to the people and cultures in which they take place.

One thing we need to be clear on is that fresh expressions are not better than the existing church. They complement it and are birthed alongside it. Existing churches may connect with people on their fringe, while many fresh expressions serve people well beyond the fringe. Both types of church can affirm and support each other in partnership – this is what's known as the "mixed economy" church.

How do they work?

Fresh expressions often emerge prayerfully through the stages in the diagram below. Each stage has its own value for the Kingdom.

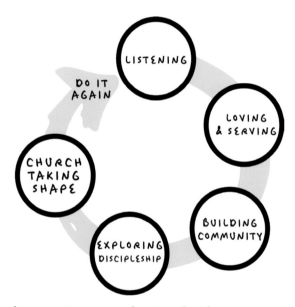

Fresh expressions are underpinned with prayer, ongoing listening, and relationship with the wider church.

They start with careful listening.

"Stepping Stones" (a fresh expression) began with some Christians asking how they could lovingly serve families in their toddler group. They held beach picnics, dads' curry nights and mums' pamper evenings.[9]

Other groups offer different forms of loving and serving. Examples include:

- A language cafe for foreigners to learn English as a second language.
- All-age events with a meal.
- Initiatives for walkers, people playing sport, and unemployed people.
- A Christian community developed on a social media platform.
- A knitting group.
- Witnessing communities in the workplace.

As Christians begin loving others in their normal everyday life, they build community with them.

Then, if appropriate, they begin to share Jesus and provide opportunities for individuals to explore becoming his disciples.

As individuals come to faith, a worshipping community with the taste of church takes shape round them. Often the community is partnered with a local church, and becomes a new congregation in effect – a mission church sent out from the existing church.

When healthy and working correctly, these new Christian communities then repeat the process, starting further fresh expressions. "Stepping Stones" grew so much that it split into two.

Of course real life is messier than diagrams! The circles usually overlap and may be taken in a different order. We'll look at that in more detail later.

Practical mission

Fresh expressions are great for mission, but are not the only approach. Their leaders say that a third of people at their main meeting once went to church but had stopped; two fifths have very little church background.[10] So most of those connecting with fresh expressions are from outside the church!

Most have yet to find faith, but a number have begun the journey. Lives are being transformed!

one third once went to church
but had stopped

two fifths had very little
church background

What needs do you see in your community? List them.

What are ways that you and your friends can begin meeting the needs of those outside the walls of the church?

Listening is a key component to starting a fresh expression and living missionally. Who do you need to listen to this week?

Who needs to be heard so that Jesus' Kingdom can come close?

4

How to start

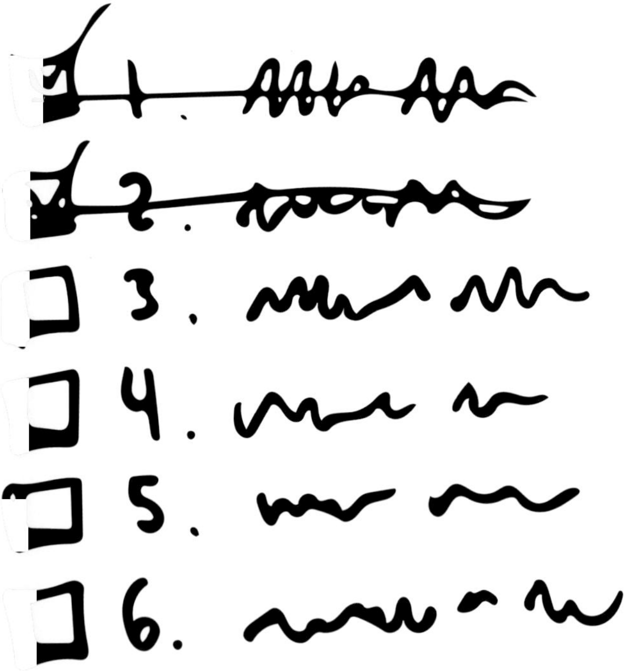
1.
2.
3.
4.
5.
6.

Step 1
Ask another Christian

God wants us to work in teams. It's part of His grand design and strategy. That's why Jesus sent out His disciples in pairs (Luke 10:1). So if you want to a start a fresh expression of church, prayerfully find someone to do it with.

Step 2
Begin with what you've got

Who are you? What do you know? Who do you know? What do you have?

What are your passions and interests? Cooking? Photography? Football?

What do you know about? Mending bikes? Building websites?

Who could you share your passion with? Who could you ask to help? For example, say you go cycling with friends. Could you ask two other Christians to organize food for the cyclists (and their partners?) when you get back? Then you'll be able to share your lives more deeply together.

What do you possess? A home to meet in? A car to transport people? Time to spend with others?

In short, what have you got in your hands and whose hands do you shake?

These are all unique gifts, skills, and experiences that God has given you to leverage for His Kingdom.

And don't forget: we don't just have to be on the giving end, other people can serve you as well.

Take Louise…

- **Who was she?** A health visitor from a local doctor's office.
- **What did she know?** That an unusually high number of young mothers suffered from post-natal depression.
- **Who did she know?** Charlie and Charlotte. They lived in the same neighbourhood as many of the mums. In a conversation, the three of them came up with the idea of starting a support group for new mothers.
- **What did they have?** Charlie and Charlotte's home, which was where the support group first met. In time, the group evolved into a Christian community.[11]

step 3
Chat to others

Speak to God directly in prayer, to those you are seeking to serve, and to others with wisdom to share. Listen and learn all you can. All it takes is for you to initiate.

For example, freshexpressions.org.uk/stories contains over 200 stories of fresh expressions, often with contact details. Why not get in touch with someone doing the type of thing you have in mind?

Don't short change this listening! If you really want to serve people around you, use conversations with them to learn and then propel you forward on the journey.

"Hot Chocolate" started with a small group of Christians offering cups of hot chocolate to young people in the centre of Dundee. As they got to know each other, the young people described how they were looking for a place for their band to rehearse (a need they had). The Christians offered them the church building (something they possessed to fulfil the need).

That was the beginning of what became a thriving community, with a worshipping core. It started with what the Christians knew – how to make hot chocolate! But it developed because they listened to the young people and responded to them.[12]

step 4
Dream up lots of possibilities

Keep asking "What if…?" "What if we did this?" "What if we did that?" Then ask, "Why not?"

"What if?" leads on to "why not?", which takes you to another "What if…?" Eventually, through prayer and seeking the answers to these questions, you will come up with a place to start.

Expert designers keep exploring possibilities. Inexperienced ones miss out on creative ideas because they narrow down options too early.[13]

step 5
Experiment like crazy

Don't be shy about trying something to see if it works. Take a risk. If it fails, start over. You have nothing to lose and everything to gain. What's the worst that could happen? It fails? There is so much freedom in starting something new for Jesus as you be church in your everyday life.

Step 6
Follow the fresh expressions journey

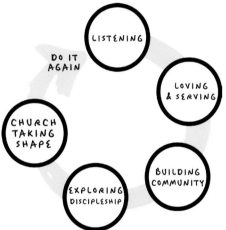

- Listen to God and the people you are called to serve.
- Find a way to love and serve the people around you.
- Build community with those you serve.
- Offer opportunities for individuals to explore becoming disciples of Jesus.
- Let a Christian community, a congregation or church, take shape round those coming to faith.
- Encourage new believers to do it again by leading others on a similar journey.

Off the top of your head, work your way through the fresh expressions journey steps and make notes in the space below. Read each step on the previous page and ask yourself what each step might look like in your context. No one will hold you to what you write here; we just want to get your creative juices flowing!

1.
2.
3.
4.
5.
6.

What do you know?
What do you have?
What are you experienced in?
What are you passionate about?
What can you absolutely not stand?

Might these be things God has given you to leverage for His Kingdom and others round you in your community?

Take some time to prayerfully reflect with God about how He has wired you, what He wants to use you for, and how to start shaking things up for Him.

5

How to be about making disciples

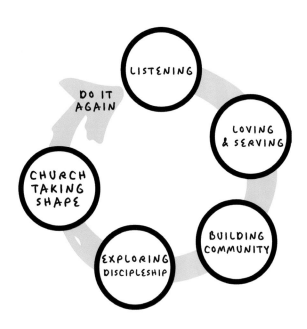

Find a framework

Jesus called His followers to make disciples (Matthew 28:19). "A fresh expressions journey" offers a framework for this. The first three circles have intrinsic value for the Kingdom, but also create opportunities for individuals to explore Jesus.

The leaders of St Laurence Church, Reading, knew lots of young people with little church background, but few were coming to faith.

A senior church leader invited them to draw what they were trying to do. The diagram ended up rather similar to "A fresh expressions journey".

The first two steps were working well, but the leaders realised they weren't creating opportunities to discover Jesus. So they started weekends away to fill this gap — a weekend all about discovering Jesus. From these sprang a worshipping community of nearly 50 young people.

Their framework enabled the leaders to see where they were going, filter out ideas that didn't fit and spot the gaps. For example, they saw it was quite a leap from "clubs" to the weekend away. Could they put in some smaller steps?[14]

Put in stepping stones to exploring discipleship

By starting a distinct group for this purpose…

It could be starting a "spirituality group" to explore topics of significance and meaning from a Christian perspective. You might explain, "We discuss stories told by Jesus, who is widely regarded as one of the world's greatest spiritual teachers, and see if we agree with them."

Alongside Xpressions Cafe are family activities and a discussion group, both on a Christian theme. They are followed by a short act of worship. Individuals can dip into what they are comfortable with.[15]

Prayer can spark conversations about Jesus. In a language cafe, ethnic women met for tea and discussed topics to practise their English. They were invited to pin prayer requests to a board. Soon they were talking about their requests! So an enquirers group was formed to explore further.[16]

The point of these groups is to create a space to meet people where they are at and to begin to engage them in spiritual conversations on their level. These new groups will be the stepping-stones to them exploring discipleship in a relaxed way that speaks their language.

By inviting enquirers to the core team...

In Gloucester, half-a-dozen Christians hosted a monthly Sunday breakfast for up to 60 people from the neighbourhood, and a variety of other activities, including a soccer team. If asked, they talked about their faith.

Anyone showing interest was invited to the planning group, which met regularly over a meal to pray, plan, and discuss the Bible. Visitors could come once or every time. Within three years, the team had grown to 18 people and multiplied into two groups.[17]

Personal evangelism can be easy. No need to fear questions like, "Why did God allow that disaster?" Christians can reply, "It's a question I struggle with, too. We sometimes talk about it in the team. Would you like to visit our next meeting? We eat together, do some planning, discuss stories about Jesus and pray in any way that makes us feel comfortable – no pressure. Join in as you like!"

"Everyone is welcome, all are participants, let's journey together and bring what we all can to the table" – this is the ethos you are trying to create by inviting others to the core team.

By involving everyone…

"Eleven Alive" has fluid and varied worship in the morning. Every two months the community enjoys a shared lunch and then breaks into 4 teams. Each team prepares the worship for two occasions over the next 8 weeks. Importantly, anyone in the community – from atheists to Christians – can join a team! This has been highly fruitful in making disciples.[18]

Share stories about Jesus

When people attend one of your stepping stones, such as an enquirers group, you can introduce Jesus by discussing Gospel stories about Him, including stories He told.

You might ask:

- If that story happened today, what would it look like?
- What does it mean to you?
- How could it make a difference to your life?

Above all, be a good friend!

Don't force people to explore Jesus if they don't wish to, or more quickly than they want. Remember, they are not a project for you to convert, but rather a friend to display God's love to… you can be Jesus to them. Learn to be patient, pray, and trust the Holy Spirit.

Let's make another list. Fill in the list below with the names of friends you have who don't yet know Jesus.

1.
2.
3.
4.
5.

What do these friends all have in common? Are there any shared interests or things that could unite you all?

What could be natural stepping stones to bring these friends together so that you can lovingly serve them and help them to explore Jesus?

What is a natural and relevant way for you to be a good friend to them as you show them Christ's love?

6

How to grow mature disciples

Be a good companion

This could be as a friend, mentor or leader. New believers may have little Christian background and their faith journey may be very different to yours. So be understanding. Walk at their pace. Remember how patient the Holy Spirit is with you, and be patient with them. Don't be an expert, but a fellow disciple… no one cares for a "know it all".

Let the community do the talking

Teachers know that pupils learn from the "hidden curriculum" – relationships and values – as much as from the official curriculum.

Your community's "hidden curriculum" is its common life and values. What are they teaching new believers that is not explicitly said?

One community invited everyone to contribute to its shared meal, including those on benefits. They wanted to show that each person had something to offer.[19] That they were all on the same footing.

Encourage conversations about Jesus

People learn by asking questions, putting what they've learnt into their own words, trying out ideas and listening to other people's comments. How can you help them self-discover?

Jesus did not merely preach at people. He taught through conversations and left room for dialogue (Mark 8:27–30; 10:17–31; John 6:25–59). So allow plenty of time for discussion.

BI, in Birmingham, invited adults to read a Bible passage in advance and discuss it with their children. When the community met, age-based groups shared what they had learnt.[20]

Couple worship to life

The Spirit works through worship that engages with everyday life and experiences. So as you introduce new Christians to worship, ask them whether it connects with their lives. Ask, too, how their daily experiences can lead to worship. What would it look like to lead a life of worship?

The worship of one fresh expression followed this sequence:

- *Gathering* – songs and prayers as people gather round Jesus.
- *Introducing* the theme – e.g. Bible passage and short talk.
- *Exploring* the theme – groups choose between discussing on social media, writing an email to a friend, composing a song, or using art to explore it.
- *Turning to God* – feedback from groups is turned into prayer to God, sometimes communion is shared.

Keep your worship:

- Simple – e.g. as part of a shared meal.
- Helpful – relevant to life.
- Authentic – e.g. using language from the heart.
- Rich – vary the diet.
- Enabling – are worshippers pooling their gifts?

Communal practices

These are activities done together to support individuals' walk with Jesus. People can do them for a limited time, either as a whole gathering or in self-selecting groups.

Examples might include:

- For six weeks, each person does one act of generosity a week and shares with the group how they got on.
- As a form of prayer, one group writes protest letters on behalf of Amnesty International (as Just Church did in Bradford);[21] another two groups write on behalf of other organisations.
- Three or four people contract to eat more healthily or to read an evening Bible story to their children.
- Each evening in Lent, individuals say the same texted prayer of confession in their homes.
- Individuals text each other prayer messages through the week.

Connect with the wider church

Christians are baptised into the whole body, and discipleship involves learning from and contributing to it. Therefore, connecting with the wider church – the greater body – brings fullness to a fresh expression.

Connecting up can include:
- Shared learning, missional, social, and worship events with another local church.
- Attending a Christian festival or conference.
- Downloading online Christian resources.
- "Blending church" by worshipping in your fresh expression and, periodically, in the church you came from.
- Getting involved with a Christian project overseas.

Picture your community as a circle, not rows

Shared leadership involves being part of the circle, inviting others to pool their gifts and mature into leadership.

One person resolved that as she read Scripture with enquirers, she would avoid answering their questions where possible. If someone asked, "Who was John the Baptist?" she would invite the group to Google the answer. The group would learn to depend not on her, but on one another led by the Spirit.

Remember, the goal here is to walk alongside other people in their discipleship journey with Jesus. As they grow and mature in their relationship to Him, you should practice giving them more responsibility for and in the group – ownership is key in fighting against a culture of consumerism in your fresh expression.

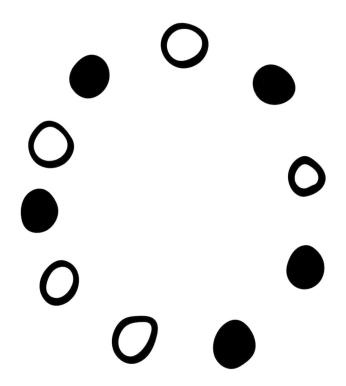

What would you say is the "hidden curriculum" that you want any group you are part of to have?

Have you ever experienced community as a circle? What made it different? What did you like/dislike?

Christians are notorious for telling and not listening. We tell people what they need to know, but don't really listen very well. Think about the people you listed in the last chapter. What is your next step to engaging them in conversation about Jesus?

What questions can you ask them?

What would it look like to take the lead and initiate with them?

7

Reproducing your fresh expression

4 REASONS

A healthy fresh expression multiplies. Disciples are matured, leaders are given a chance to grow, take ownership, and lead, and, in time, it is ready to birth something new for the Kingdom again. Here are four reasons why reproduction is essential…

#1 God wants believers to be missional through the week within Christian communities, not just out on their own trying to do it themselves – as we saw in Chapter 2.

If that's true for those who begin a fresh expression, it must also be true for people who find faith through one. They too must learn to be and do mission in community. Launching out to start another fresh expression can help them with this.

#2 Throughout history the church has spread by reproducing. In Acts, new believers led the way. Jews from Cyprus and Cyrene came to Jerusalem, discovered Jesus, were forced to leave because of persecution and travelled to Antioch, where they started a church (Acts 2:10; 11:20).

If recent converts founded Christian communities then, why not today?

71

#3 Multiplying is the best way for fresh expressions to grow. Often Christian communities expand quickly, then plateau. You can avoid this levelling off by starting a further community.

A church worker formed a Christian community in her front room with people on a council estate. Space became tight. But instead of starting a second group in another home, they moved to a nearby school.

Big mistake!

Many on the estate had hated school! Though new families from the school came, the originals drifted away. Multiplying small groups might have been better than trying to grow a large one. Bigger is not always better in the Kingdom.

#4 Reproducing is more important than creating a durable fresh expression. Some fresh expressions may last a long time, others for a season. The Holy Spirit can be in both.

The Jerusalem church existed for a relatively short period – until AD 70, when the city was destroyed. But it was highly fruitful. Scores of Jews had visited Jerusalem, heard about Jesus, gone home and started church – as far away as Rome. Fruitfulness is more important than sustainability.

Three principles for reproducing...

Encourage the right expectation

As individuals come to faith, help them see that multiplying expressions of church is part of the Christian life. It's completely normal and will be their new normal as they experience this for themselves.

For example, when you explain what it means to be a Christian, why not say that it may involve finding one or more Christians, together loving and serving the people nearby, creating community with those being served, sharing Jesus as appropriate, and seeing what the Spirit does – "just as we have done with you". Enquirers will enter the faith with that possibility in mind.

Keep things simple

As you introduce people to Jesus, prayerfully use approaches they can easily copy. Show DVDs they can share with their contacts. Use forms of "discovery" Bible study they can easily adapt, perhaps based on these questions:

- What would this story look like if it happened today?
- What does it mean to you?
- How could it make a difference to your life?

Find ways of praying that emerging Christians could show their friends. The same applies to worship. People are shy about singing? Why not listen to Christian songs?

Mentor new believers

Invite them to take you into their world and explore how the earlier chapter on "How to Start" might work for them. Modelling it for them is key. Perhaps you can help them to think through how to get started in their own context?

Two examples...

Parents and carers in Cambridge came to faith through a discussion group for people who had dropped their children at school. They were enthused about what they were experiencing and wanted to invite their friends. But their friends were at work. So they started "Thirst Too" on Saturday afternoons for the people they knew.[22]

"Sorted" began among eleven to fourteen-year-olds. As the group got older they asked their leaders, "Why don't we do with the next generation what you did with us?" And they did![23]

Why do we think bigger is better when it comes to church in our culture? Is this accurate?

Think for a moment about the human life cycle. What comparisons can you draw out from this and a healthy life cycle of a church/fresh expression?

Expectations of the group are everything in multiplying your fresh expression. What are some words/phrases you would use to describe this reproduction idea to a new member of your group?

Jot them down here:

8

How to measure fruitfulness

Evaluating fresh expressions is about discerning what the Spirit is up to. It is not mainly about targets. It is about recognizing what the Spirit has been doing and what you are called to do next. Here are some key principles that will help you to measure the fruit of your fresh expression.

Embed it in your praying

Evaluation should be continuous, not something you do every so often. So include it whenever you pray and plan.

Indeed, evaluation can be a framework for your praying and planning. Base it on these questions:

- *What is going on*? Where have we got to? What happened since we last met? Offer your answers prayerfully to God.
- *What could be?* What are possible next steps? Ask God to stretch your imagination.
- *What will be?* Agree who will do what, when. Seek God's help.

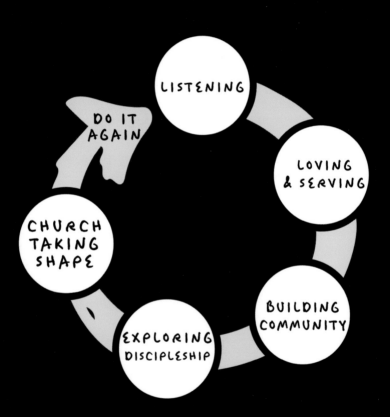

Every now and again, pray about these same "discernment questions" in relation to the journey.

- *What is going on?* What stage of the journey have we reached?
- *What could be?* What are possible steps to the next stage?
- *What will be?* Which of these steps shall we focus on?

If you oversee a fresh expression on behalf of your parent church or denomination, these questions can be a simple and effective form of accountability. You can discuss them with the community's leaders so that you are all on the same page.

You will be measuring fruitfulness not simply as "bums on seats", but as progress along a path.

Reducing fruitfulness to numbers will always be difficult. What is a satisfactory number? Jesus said the Kingdom is like a mustard seed (Matthew 13:31): a fresh expression may look small, but become highly fruitful. Many conventional congregations are tiny. So we must beware of judging success by size.

It is better to see success as movement toward a destination. "A fresh expressions journey" enables you to recognize movement from one milestone to another.

If together you set targets – "reach the next stage of the journey in twelve months" – be flexible. The Spirit is full of surprises and may have other ideas!

Remember:
The journey may be more difficult than you realize.

Fresh expressions often grow by responding to unexpected opportunities.

> The Ark play centre and cafe had this experience – they said "The church side of the Ark keeps taking us in surprising directions!"[24]

Beware of being so keen to hit a target that you hurry through the vital process of listening – "We can't keep listening to the context. We must show we've started something." With this approach, a lack of "market research" can mean that the initiative flounders as it isn't right for the context.[25]

Evaluate growth in discipleship

As the fresh expression nears the left-hand side of the journey on page 80, you will focus more on maturity. How can you measure spiritual growth?

You might do so by thinking about each of the interlocking relationships at the heart of church:

- UP – with God
- IN – within the fellowship
- OUT – with the world
- OF – with the wider church (part *of* the whole body)

Once a year, you might ask the three "discernment questions" in relation to each set of relationships – for example, for UP:

- *What is going on?* What are the strengths and weaknesses of the community's current relationship with God? Have we achieved the goals we set a year ago (e.g. to run a short course on the Gospels)? What was the impact?
- *What could be?* What might we seek to achieve in the next 12 months?
- *What will be?* Which of these possibilities shall we go for?

You can then continue by asking these questions for each of the remaining interlocking relationships – IN, OUT, OF. This will provide a framework for setting goals and evaluating the results. But again: don't be a slave to your goals! The Spirit may unfold something new.

Might more conventional churches use a similar approach to help them to plan and review initiatives and ministries?

What do you think it means to measure fruitfulness by faithfulness?

Based on this chapter, how would you describe the "ideal" fresh expression? What characterizes it? What does it look like? How does it behave? What does it value?

As you think about leading or being involved in a fresh expression, what three words would you use to describe what you hope to see?

1.

2.

3.

9

Now
what?

YOUR TURN

Now it's your turn.

Prayerfully breathe in the words in this book. They have the potential to change everything for you.

God has uniquely wired you, supernaturally gifted you, and given you experiences, skills, and passions to be leveraged for His Kingdom. Beyond that, He has placed you exactly where He wants you in this season of your life. Might it be time to jump out of the boat and begin the fresh expressions journey?

The church in the West is in desperate need of a fresh wave of life. Yes, we need prayer in abundance to see our countries revived in the name of Jesus, but we also need people – willing people who care more about the glory of God than their own personal comfort…

People who have been shaken by the Spirit to start something for God…

People who have caught the vision for Christian communities in every segment of life…

People who are ready to make Jesus tangibly present in a world far from Him…

Might this be you?

This is an invitation – one that was extended the moment you met Jesus. So why not partner with Him and change the course of history, not only for yourself... but also for the people around you?

It's your move. What's it going to be?

Additional resources from the authors

Rev Dr Michael Moynagh:

Being Church Doing Life: Creating gospel communities where life happens

Church for Every Context: An Introduction to Theology and Practice

Rob Peabody:

Citizen – Your role in the alternative kingdom
citizenthebook.com

Intersect – Where your story and God's story converge
intersectseries.com

About the authors

The **Revd Dr Michael Moynagh** is based at Wycliffe Hall, Oxford, and is the author of several books about new kinds of Christian community. His *Church for Every Context* is a leading academic text on the fresh expressions movement. He is a consultant on theology and practice to the UK's Fresh Expressions team, and is is a recognized authority on new types of church.

Rob Peabody serves as the Co-Founder and CEO of Awaken, a non-profit charity that exists to resource the church for action. In 2011, Rob left his position as lead campus pastor of a megachurch in Texas to pioneer and lead fresh expressions of church seeking to engage unreached 20s and 30s in northeast London. He currently serves as the Global City Leader for London for the International Mission Board, and heads up Fresh Expressions pioneering efforts amongst the next generation.

Notes

1 Acts 2; Acts 4

2 Acts 2:47

3 Acts 18:23–41

4 www.freshexpressions.org.uk/stories/legacyxs

5 www.freshexpressions.org.uk/stories/saturdaygathering

6 George Lings to Michael Moynagh/Norman Ivison, email, 21 March 2014; Church Army Research Unit, *An analysis of fresh expressions of church and church plants begun in the period 1992–2012*, Church Army/Church of England: 2013, p. 6.

7 George Lings to Michael Moynagh/Norman Ivison, email, 21 March 2014.

8 www.freshexpressions.org.uk/stories/cookatchapel/feb14

9 Sheila Porter to Michael Moynagh, email, 12 January 2015.

10 Church Army Research Unit, *An analysis of fresh expressions of church and church plants begun in the period 1992–2012*, Church Army/Church of England: 2013, p. 6.

11 See www.freshexpressions.org.uk/stories/kairos

12 www.freshexpressions.org.uk/stories/hotchocolate

13 Nigel Cross, *Design Thinking*, London: Bloomsbury, 2011.

14 Chris Russell to Michael Moynagh, email, 18 December 2014.

15 www.freshexpressions.org.uk/stories/xpressions/oct14

16 Caroline Newbolt to Michael Moynagh, email, 5 January 2015.

17 Ian Meredith to Michael Moynagh, email, 23 December 2014.

18 Interview with Tim Mitchell, 16 October 2014.

19 Felicity Vincent to Michael Moynagh, email, 7 January 2015.

20 www.freshexpressions.org.uk/stories/B1.
21 Chris Howson, *A Just Church: 21st Century Liberation Theology in Action*, London: Continuum, 2011.
22 www.freshexpressions.org.uk/stories/thirsttoo
23 www.freshexpressions.org.uk/stories/sorted/nov15
24 www.freshexpressions.org.uk/stories/arkcrawcook/oct14
25 You can further explore this approach to accountability, including sample questions, in Michael Moynagh, *Being Church, Doing Life*, pp. 319–44